LIVE MORE LIKE
BUDDHA

Guidance and wisdom from
the enlightened one

LIVE MORE LIKE BUDDHA

Summersdale Publishers Ltd
46 West Street
Chichester
West Sussex
PO19 1RP
UK

www.summersdale.com

Printed and bound in the Czech Republic

ISBN: 978-1-84953-712-4

TO my dearest friend
with all my love
FROM Tracey XXX.
Happy 50th Birthday

IF ANYTHING IS WORTH DOING, DO IT WITH ALL YOUR HEART.

Health is the greatest gift,
contentment is the greatest wealth,
a trusted friend is the best relative.

If for company you cannot find a wise and prudent friend who leads a good life, then… like a lone elephant in the elephant forest, you should go your way alone.

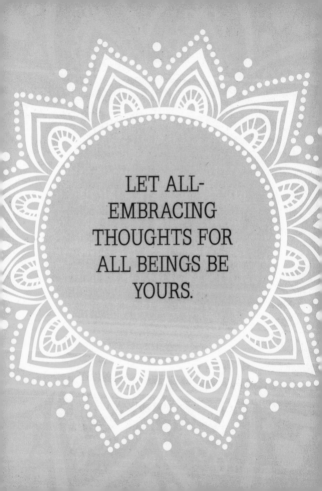

LET ALL-
EMBRACING
THOUGHTS FOR
ALL BEINGS BE
YOURS.

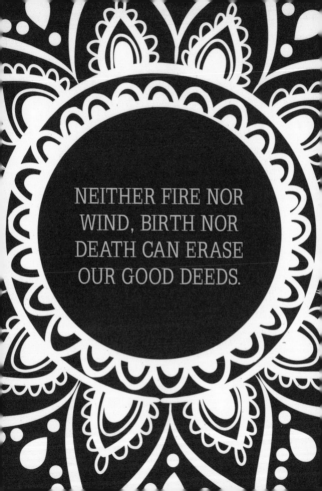

NEITHER FIRE NOR WIND, BIRTH NOR DEATH CAN ERASE OUR GOOD DEEDS.

There are these three things
which shine forth for all to see,
which are not hidden. Which three?
The disc of the moon shines for
all to see; it is not hidden. The
disc of the sun does likewise.
The truth of a Buddha shines
for all to see; it is not hidden.

If with an impure mind a person speaks or acts, suffering follows him like the wheel that follows the foot of the ox.

IF A MAN SPEAKS
OR ACTS WITH A
PURE THOUGHT,
HAPPINESS
FOLLOWS HIM,
LIKE A SHADOW
THAT NEVER
LEAVES HIM.

You live for the good of both
– your own, the other's –

when, knowing the other's
provoked, you mindfully grow calm.

HE WHO REPAYS AN
ANGRY MAN IN KIND
IS WORSE THAN THE
ANGRY MAN.

To keep the body in good health is a duty, for otherwise we shall not be able to trim the lamp of wisdom, and keep our minds strong and clear.

Searching all directions with your awareness, you find no one dearer than yourself. In the same way, others are thickly dear to themselves. So you shouldn't hurt others if you love yourself.

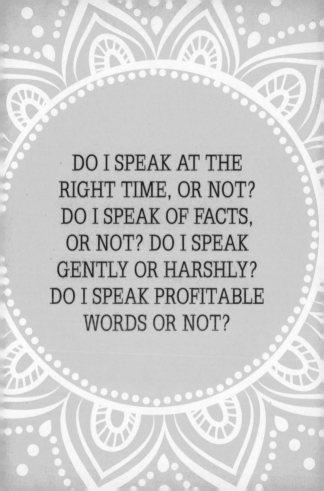

DO I SPEAK AT THE
RIGHT TIME, OR NOT?
DO I SPEAK OF FACTS,
OR NOT? DO I SPEAK
GENTLY OR HARSHLY?
DO I SPEAK PROFITABLE
WORDS OR NOT?

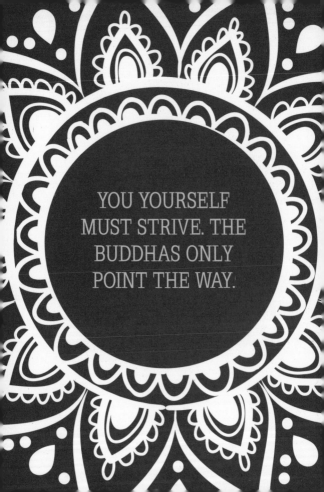

YOU YOURSELF
MUST STRIVE. THE
BUDDHAS ONLY
POINT THE WAY.

There are these five seasonable gifts. Which five? One gives to a newcomer. One gives to one going away. One gives to one who is ill. One gives in time of famine. One sets the first fruits of field and orchard in front of those who are virtuous.

Don't go by reports, by legends, by traditions, by scripture, by logical conjecture, by inference, by analogies, by agreement through pondering views, by probability, or by the thought, 'This contemplative is our teacher.'

ONE TRIES TO ABANDON WRONG SPEECH AND TO ENTER INTO RIGHT SPEECH: THIS IS ONE'S RIGHT EFFORT.

Do not speak harshly to anyone.
Those who are harshly spoken
to might retaliate against you.

Angry words hurt others'
feelings, even blows may
overtake you in return.

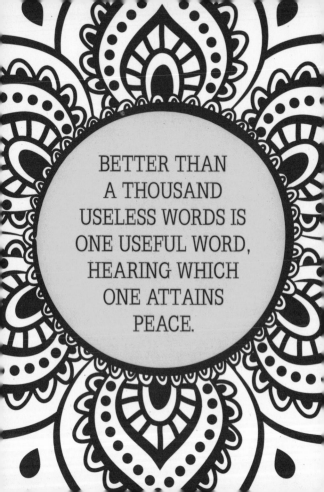

BETTER THAN
A THOUSAND
USELESS WORDS IS
ONE USEFUL WORD,
HEARING WHICH
ONE ATTAINS
PEACE.

Five blessings, householders,
accrue to the righteous person
through his practice of virtue: great
increase of wealth through his
diligence; a favourable reputation;
a confident deportment, without
timidity... a serene death; and,
at the breaking up of the body
after death, rebirth in a happy
state, in a heavenly world.

Heedfulness is the path
to the Deathless.
Heedlessness is the
path to death.
The heedful die not.
The heedless are as
if dead already.

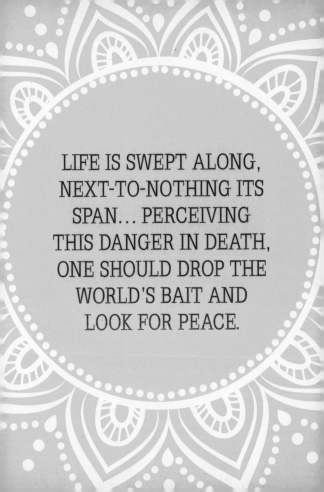

LIFE IS SWEPT ALONG,
NEXT-TO-NOTHING ITS
SPAN... PERCEIVING
THIS DANGER IN DEATH,
ONE SHOULD DROP THE
WORLD'S BAIT AND
LOOK FOR PEACE.

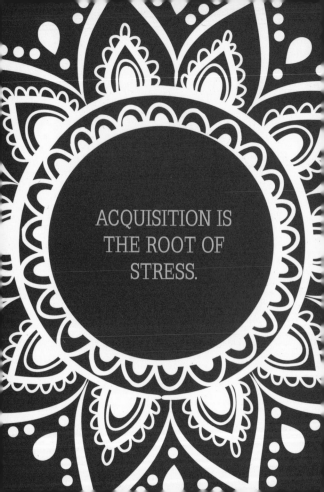

ACQUISITION IS
THE ROOT OF
STRESS.

Free from anger and untroubled,
free from greed, without longing,
tamed, your anger abandoned,
free from fermentation,
you will be unbound.

As a water bead on a lotus leaf, as water on a red lily, does not adhere, so the sage does not adhere to the seen, the heard or the sensed.

GUARD YOUR
MIND AGAINST
AN OUTBURST OF
WRONG FEELINGS.
KEEP YOUR MIND
CONTROLLED.

The person who lies, who
transgress in this one thing,
transcending concern for
the world beyond:

there's no evil he might not do.

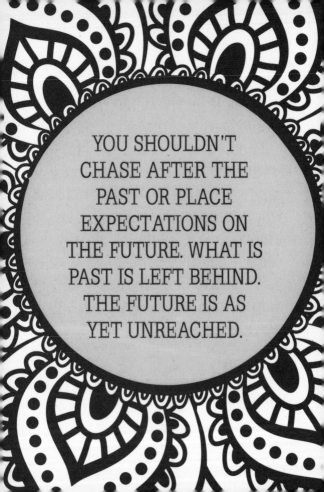

YOU SHOULDN'T
CHASE AFTER THE
PAST OR PLACE
EXPECTATIONS ON
THE FUTURE. WHAT IS
PAST IS LEFT BEHIND.
THE FUTURE IS AS
YET UNREACHED.

A disciple lets his mind pervade one quarter of the world with thoughts of unselfish joy, and so the second, and so the third, and so the fourth. And thus the whole wide world, above, below, around, everywhere and equally, he continues to pervade with a heart of unselfish joy, abundant, grown great, measureless, without hostility or ill-will.

You should [also] practise the establishment of mindfulness [by saying], 'I will look after others.'

THOSE WHO CLING
TO PERCEPTIONS
AND VIEWS
WANDER THE
WORLD OFFENDING
PEOPLE.

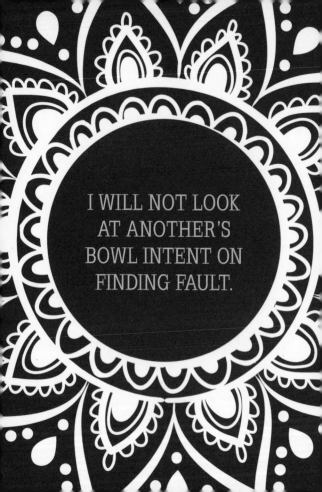

I WILL NOT LOOK
AT ANOTHER'S
BOWL INTENT ON
FINDING FAULT.

Be islands unto yourselves,
refuges unto yourselves,
seeking no external refuge.

Therefore, monks, your duty is
the contemplation, 'This is stress...
This is the origination of stress...
This is the cessation of stress.'
Your duty is the contemplation,
'This is the path of practice leading
to the cessation of stress.'

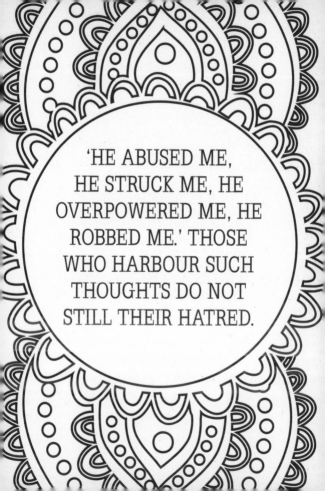

'HE ABUSED ME, HE STRUCK ME, HE OVERPOWERED ME, HE ROBBED ME.' THOSE WHO HARBOUR SUCH THOUGHTS DO NOT STILL THEIR HATRED.

Whenever you want to do a verbal
action, you should reflect on it:

'This verbal action I want to do –
would it lead to self-affliction, to
the affliction of others, or to both?'

UPON A HEAP OF
RUBBISH IN THE ROAD-
SIDE DITCH BLOOMS
A LOTUS, FRAGRANT
AND PLEASING.

These, monks, are the seven treasures. The treasure of conviction, the treasure of virtue, the treasure of conscience and concern, the treasure of listening, generosity, and discernment as the seventh treasure. Whoever, man or woman, has these treasures is said not to be poor, has not lived in vain.

When a man dwells with his heart possessed and overwhelmed by sense-desires... then he cannot know or see, as it really is, what is to his own profit, nor can he know and see what is to the profit of others, or of both himself and others.

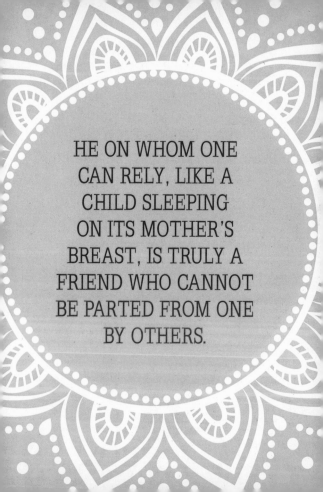

HE ON WHOM ONE
CAN RELY, LIKE A
CHILD SLEEPING
ON ITS MOTHER'S
BREAST, IS TRULY A
FRIEND WHO CANNOT
BE PARTED FROM ONE
BY OTHERS.

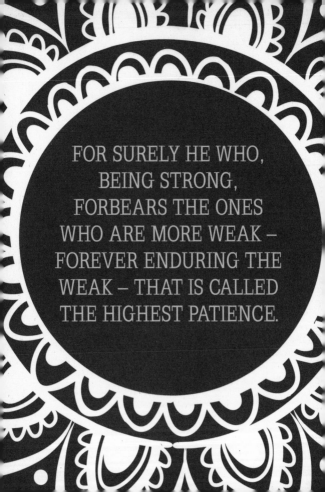

FOR SURELY HE WHO, BEING STRONG, FORBEARS THE ONES WHO ARE MORE WEAK – FOREVER ENDURING THE WEAK – THAT IS CALLED THE HIGHEST PATIENCE.

Practise jhana*... Don't be heedless. Don't later fall into regret. This is our message to you all.

*Jhana is a meditative state

This is how to contemplate
our conditioned existence
in this fleeting world:
Like a tiny drop of dew, or a
bubble floating in a stream;
Like a flash of lightning
in a summer cloud,
Or a flickering lamp, an illusion,
a phantom or a dream.
So is all conditioned
existence to be seen.

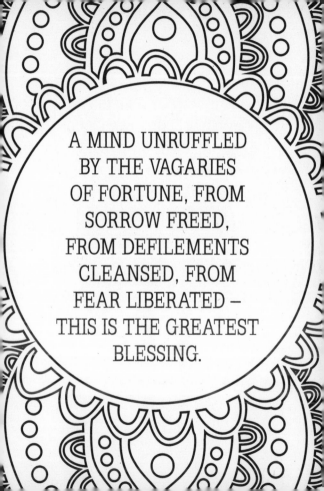

A MIND UNRUFFLED
BY THE VAGARIES
OF FORTUNE, FROM
SORROW FREED,
FROM DEFILEMENTS
CLEANSED, FROM
FEAR LIBERATED –
THIS IS THE GREATEST
BLESSING.

When anger arises, whoever
keeps firm control as if
with a racing chariot:

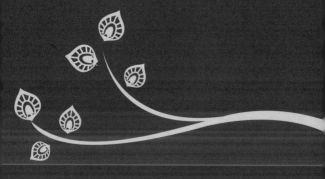

him I call a master
charioteer. Anyone else, a
rein-holder – that's all.

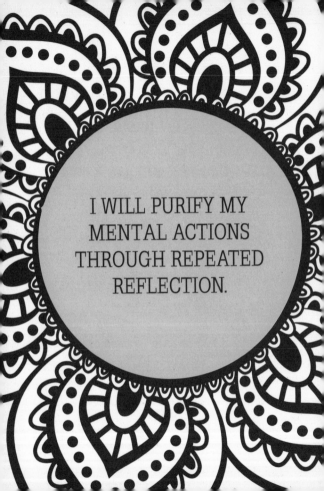

I WILL PURIFY MY MENTAL ACTIONS THROUGH REPEATED REFLECTION.

Realising that this body is
as fragile as a clay pot, and
fortifying this mind like a well-
fortified city, fight out Mara*
with the sword of wisdom.

*Mara is the Buddhist personification
of wilful ignorance

Some misguided men… learn
the Truth only for the sake of
criticising others and for winning
in debates, and they do not
experience the good for the sake of
which they learned the Dhamma*.

*Dhamma is the Truth taught by Buddha

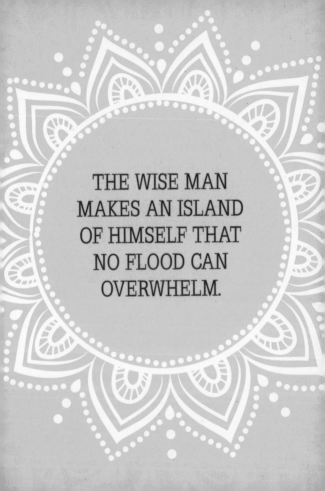

THE WISE MAN
MAKES AN ISLAND
OF HIMSELF THAT
NO FLOOD CAN
OVERWHELM.

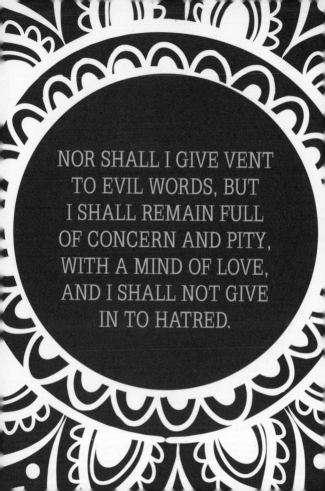

NOR SHALL I GIVE VENT
TO EVIL WORDS, BUT
I SHALL REMAIN FULL
OF CONCERN AND PITY,
WITH A MIND OF LOVE,
AND I SHALL NOT GIVE
IN TO HATRED.

How blissful it is, for one
who has nothing.
Attainers-of-wisdom are
people with nothing.
See him suffering, one
who has something,
a person bound in
mind with people.

Not at others' wrong behaviour, not
at others' things-done-or-not-done;
Only at one's own things-done-
or-not-done should one look.

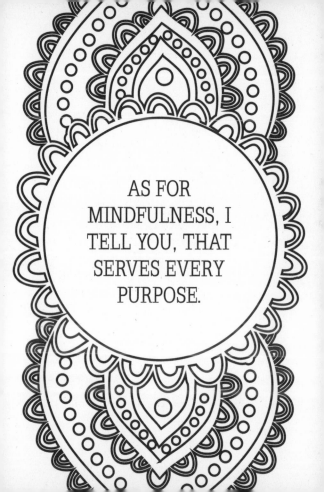

AS FOR
MINDFULNESS, I
TELL YOU, THAT
SERVES EVERY
PURPOSE.

He who is meditative, stainless
and settled, whose work is done
and who is free from cankers,

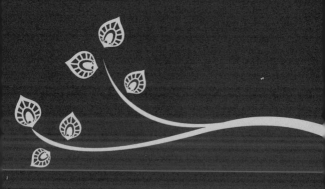

having reached the highest goal
– him do I call a holy man.

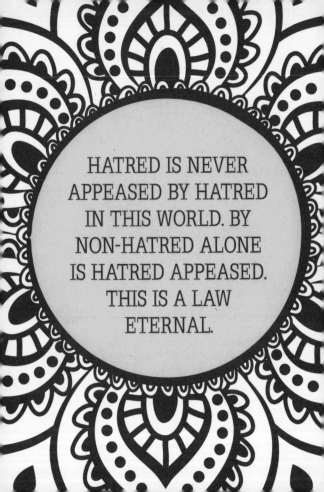

HATRED IS NEVER
APPEASED BY HATRED
IN THIS WORLD. BY
NON-HATRED ALONE
IS HATRED APPEASED.
THIS IS A LAW
ETERNAL.

They're addicted to heedlessness
– dullards, fools – while one who
is wise cherishes heedfulness
as his highest wealth.

This I tell you: decay is inherent
in all conditioned things. Work out
your own salvation, with diligence.

SPEAK ONLY THE
SPEECH THAT
NEITHER TORMENTS
SELF NOR DOES HARM
TO OTHERS. THAT
SPEECH IS TRULY
WELL SPOKEN.

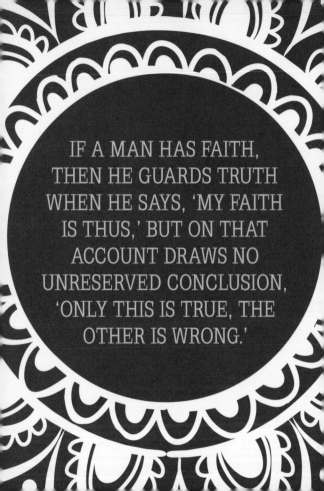

IF A MAN HAS FAITH, THEN HE GUARDS TRUTH WHEN HE SAYS, 'MY FAITH IS THUS,' BUT ON THAT ACCOUNT DRAWS NO UNRESERVED CONCLUSION, 'ONLY THIS IS TRUE, THE OTHER IS WRONG.'

When a house is on fire the vessel salvaged is the one that will be of use, not the one left there to burn. So when the world is on fire with aging and death, one should salvage [one's wealth] by giving: what's given is well salvaged.

When you know for yourselves:
These are wholesome; these things
are not blameworthy; these things
are praised by the wise; undertaken
and observed, these things lead
to benefit and happiness, having
undertaken them, abide in them.

THOUGH ALL
ONE'S LIFE A FOOL
ASSOCIATES WITH A
WISE PERSON, HE NO
MORE COMPREHENDS
THE TRUTH THAN A
SPOON TASTES THE
FLAVOUR OF
THE SOUP.

Monks, gains, offerings, and
fame are a cruel thing,

a harsh, bitter obstacle to the
attainment of the unexcelled
rest from bondage.

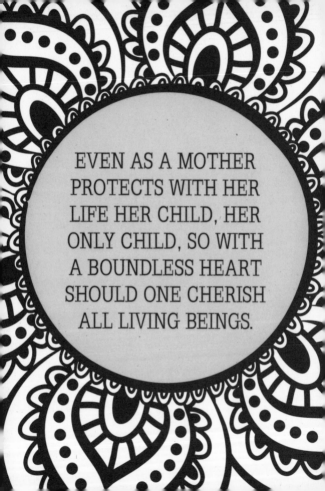

EVEN AS A MOTHER
PROTECTS WITH HER
LIFE HER CHILD, HER
ONLY CHILD, SO WITH
A BOUNDLESS HEART
SHOULD ONE CHERISH
ALL LIVING BEINGS.

The forest of restless dancing about
I've cut at the root. Though in the
forest, I'm deforested, de-arrowed. I
delight alone, discontent cast away.

He goes to hell, the one who asserts what didn't take place, as does the one who, having done, says, 'I didn't.'

TRAIN IN ACTS OF
MERIT THAT BRING
LONG-LASTING
BLISS – DEVELOP
GIVING, A LIFE IN
TUNE, A MIND OF
GOOD WILL.

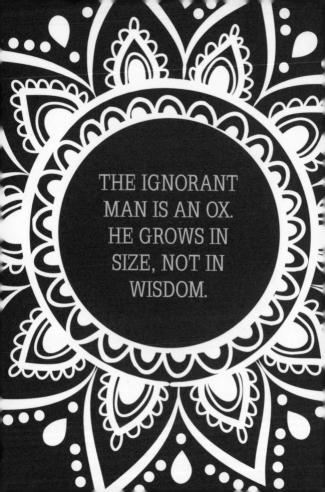

THE IGNORANT
MAN IS AN OX.
HE GROWS IN
SIZE, NOT IN
WISDOM.

Resolutely train yourself
to attain peace.

All four castes – if they refrain from taking life, from stealing, from sexual misconduct, from telling lies, from speaking divisive speech, from harsh speech, and from idle chatter, are not greedy, bear no thoughts of ill-will, and hold to right view... reappear in the good destination, the heavenly world.

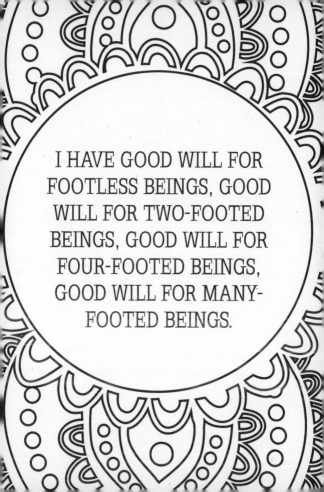

I HAVE GOOD WILL FOR FOOTLESS BEINGS, GOOD WILL FOR TWO-FOOTED BEINGS, GOOD WILL FOR FOUR-FOOTED BEINGS, GOOD WILL FOR MANY-FOOTED BEINGS.

Think not lightly of good, saying, 'It will not come to me.' Drop by drop is the water pot filled.

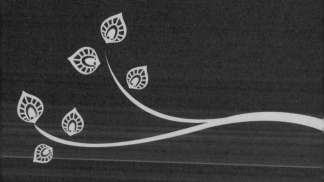

Likewise, the wise man,
gathering it little by little,
fills himself with good.

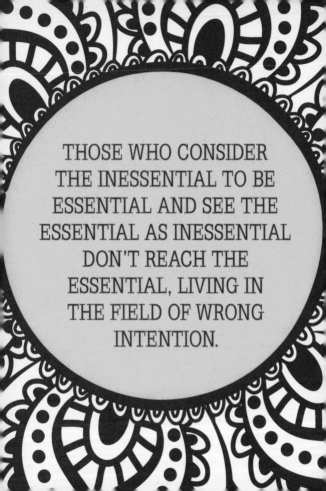

THOSE WHO CONSIDER
THE INESSENTIAL TO BE
ESSENTIAL AND SEE THE
ESSENTIAL AS INESSENTIAL
DON'T REACH THE
ESSENTIAL, LIVING IN
THE FIELD OF WRONG
INTENTION.

I having pierced through the shell of ignorance for the sake of creatures wrapped in ignorance, egg-born (as it were), am unique in the world, utterly enlightened with unsurpassed enlightenment.

But as one who's embarked
on a sturdy boat, with rudder
and oars, would – mindful,
skilful, knowing the needed
techniques – carry many others
across, even so an attainer-of-
knowledge, learned, self-developed,
unwavering can get other people
to comprehend – if they're
willing to listen, ready to learn.

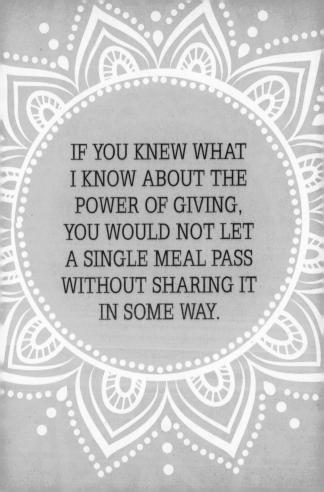

IF YOU KNEW WHAT
I KNOW ABOUT THE
POWER OF GIVING,
YOU WOULD NOT LET
A SINGLE MEAL PASS
WITHOUT SHARING IT
IN SOME WAY.

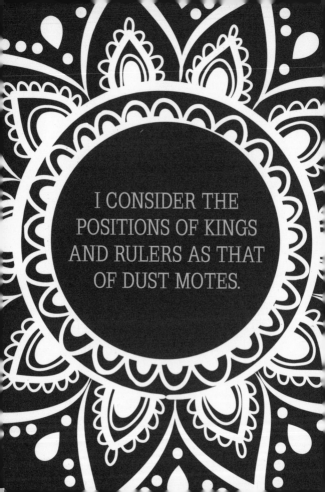

I CONSIDER THE POSITIONS OF KINGS AND RULERS AS THAT OF DUST MOTES.

Irrigators channel waters; fletchers straighten arrows; carpenters bend wood; the wise master themselves.

Few cross over the river.
Most are stranded on this side.
On the riverbank they
run up and down.

DELIGHT IN
HEEDFULNESS.
GUARD WELL YOUR
THOUGHTS.

Better it is to live one day seeing
the rise and fall of things

than to live a hundred years without
ever seeing the rise and fall of things.

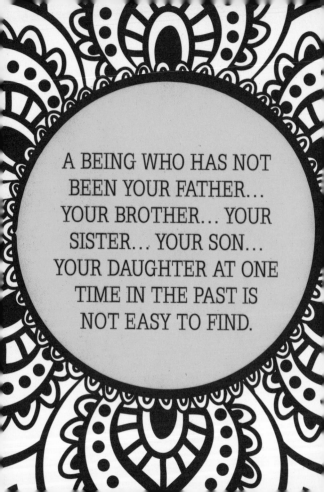

A BEING WHO HAS NOT
BEEN YOUR FATHER...
YOUR BROTHER... YOUR
SISTER... YOUR SON...
YOUR DAUGHTER AT ONE
TIME IN THE PAST IS
NOT EASY TO FIND.

In giving a meal, the donor
gives five things to the recipient.
Which five? He gives life,
beauty, happiness, strength,
and quick-wittedness.

We will develop love, we will practise it, we will make it both a way and a basis.

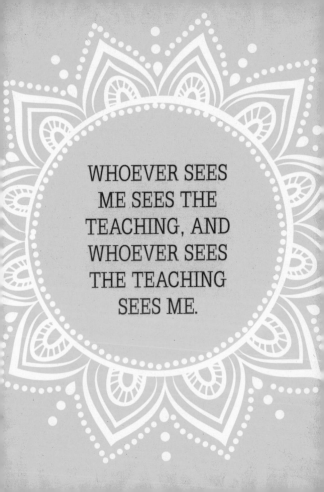

WHOEVER SEES
ME SEES THE
TEACHING, AND
WHOEVER SEES
THE TEACHING
SEES ME.

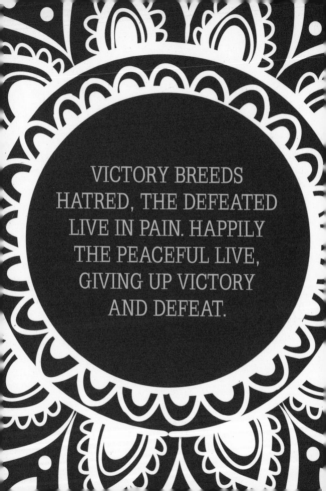

VICTORY BREEDS
HATRED, THE DEFEATED
LIVE IN PAIN. HAPPILY
THE PEACEFUL LIVE,
GIVING UP VICTORY
AND DEFEAT.

The friend who is a helper,
The friend through thick and thin,
The friend who gives good counsel,
And the compassionate friend;
These four are friends indeed.

There is the case where a person of integrity, when asked, does not reveal another person's bad points, to say nothing of when unasked… Then again, a person of integrity, when unasked, reveals another person's good points, to say nothing of when asked.

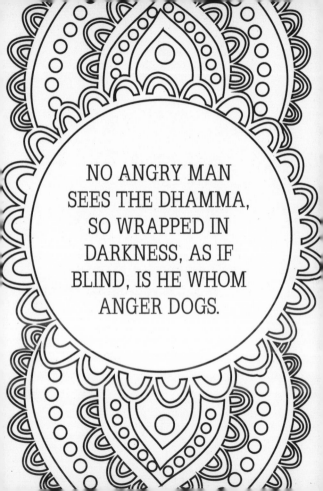

NO ANGRY MAN
SEES THE DHAMMA,
SO WRAPPED IN
DARKNESS, AS IF
BLIND, IS HE WHOM
ANGER DOGS.

There are no chains like hate...
dwelling on your brother's
faults multiplies your own.

You are far from the end
of your journey.

HASTEN TO DO
GOOD; RESTRAIN
YOUR MIND FROM
EVIL. HE WHO IS
SLOW IN DOING
GOOD, HIS MIND
DELIGHTS IN EVIL.

Let a man remove his anger. Let him root out his pride. Let him overcome all fetters of passions. No sufferings overtake him who neither clings to mind-and-body nor claims anything of the world.

A statement endowed with five factors is well-spoken, not ill-spoken… It is spoken at the right time. It is spoken in truth. It is spoken affectionately. It is spoken beneficially. It is spoken with a mind of good will.

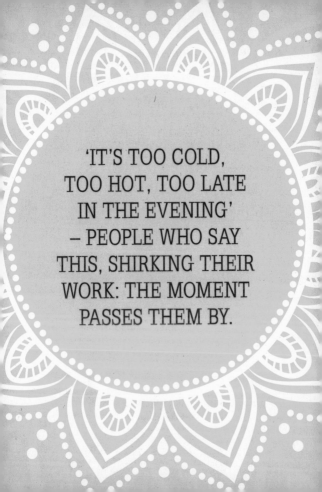

'IT'S TOO COLD,
TOO HOT, TOO LATE
IN THE EVENING'
– PEOPLE WHO SAY
THIS, SHIRKING THEIR
WORK: THE MOMENT
PASSES THEM BY.

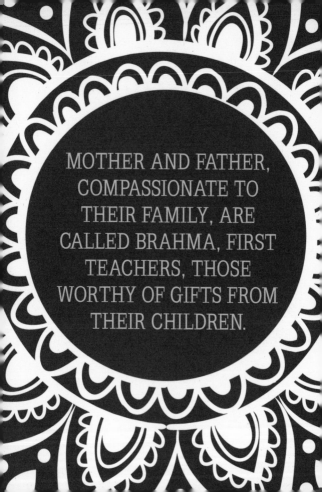

MOTHER AND FATHER, COMPASSIONATE TO THEIR FAMILY, ARE CALLED BRAHMA, FIRST TEACHERS, THOSE WORTHY OF GIFTS FROM THEIR CHILDREN.

The earth's sprinkled with rain,
wind is blowing, lightning wanders
the sky, but my thoughts are
stilled, well-centred my mind.

Overcome the angry by non-anger;
overcome the wicked by goodness;
overcome the miser by generosity;
overcome the liar by truth.

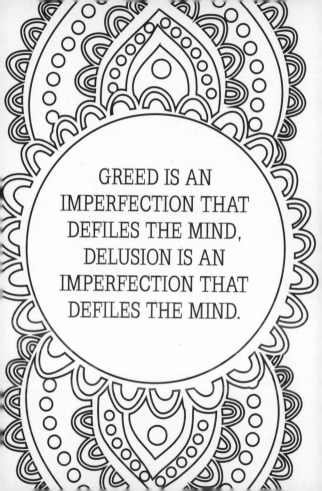

GREED IS AN
IMPERFECTION THAT
DEFILES THE MIND,
DELUSION IS AN
IMPERFECTION THAT
DEFILES THE MIND.

Monks, there are these two conditions for the arising of wrong view. Which two?

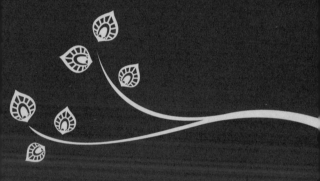

The voice of another and
inappropriate attention. These
are the two conditions for
the arising of wrong view.

WHOEVER
DOESN'T FLARE
UP AT SOMEONE
WHO'S ANGRY
WINS A BATTLE
HARD TO WIN.

These two are fools. Which two? The one who doesn't see his transgression as a transgression, and the one who doesn't rightfully pardon another who has confessed his transgression. These two are fools.

One truly is the protector of oneself;
who else could the protector be?

THE GIFT OF
TRUTH EXCELS
ALL GIFTS.

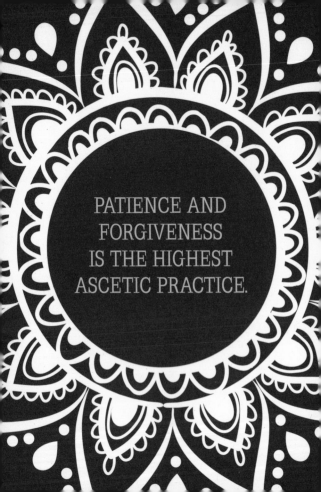

PATIENCE AND
FORGIVENESS
IS THE HIGHEST
ASCETIC PRACTICE.

Those who have come to be,
those who will be:
All will go,
leaving the body behind.
The skilful person,
realising the loss of all,
should live the holy life ardently.

When you come upon a path that
brings benefit and happiness
to all, follow this course as the
moon journeys through the stars.

MAY ALL THAT
HAVE LIFE BE
DELIVERED FROM
SUFFERING.

Looking after oneself, one
looks after others.

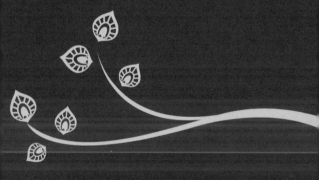

Looking after others, one
looks after oneself.

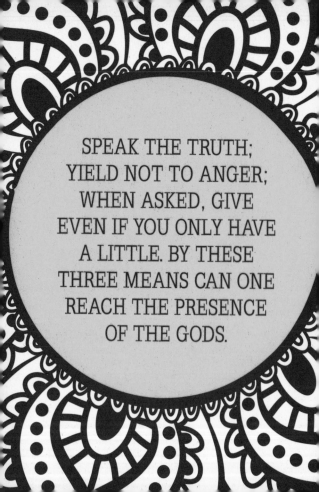

SPEAK THE TRUTH;
YIELD NOT TO ANGER;
WHEN ASKED, GIVE
EVEN IF YOU ONLY HAVE
A LITTLE. BY THESE
THREE MEANS CAN ONE
REACH THE PRESENCE
OF THE GODS.

If a traveller does not meet with one who is his better, or his equal, let him firmly keep to his solitary journey; there is no companionship with a fool.

What, my friends, is the root of evil? Desire is the root of evil; hatred is the root of evil; illusion is the root of evil.

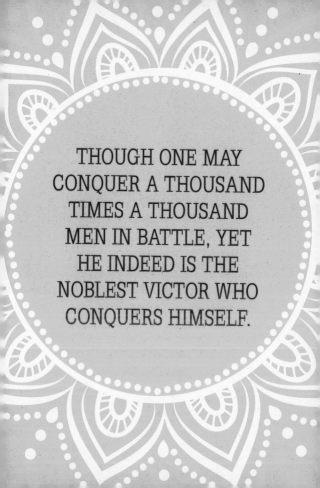

THOUGH ONE MAY
CONQUER A THOUSAND
TIMES A THOUSAND
MEN IN BATTLE, YET
HE INDEED IS THE
NOBLEST VICTOR WHO
CONQUERS HIMSELF.

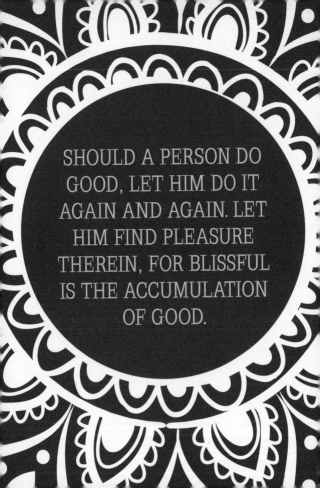

SHOULD A PERSON DO GOOD, LET HIM DO IT AGAIN AND AGAIN. LET HIM FIND PLEASURE THEREIN, FOR BLISSFUL IS THE ACCUMULATION OF GOOD.

I am the owner of my actions, heir to my actions, born of my actions, related through my actions, and have my actions as my arbitrator.

As rain falls equally on the just and the unjust, do not burden your heart with judgements but rain your kindness equally on all.

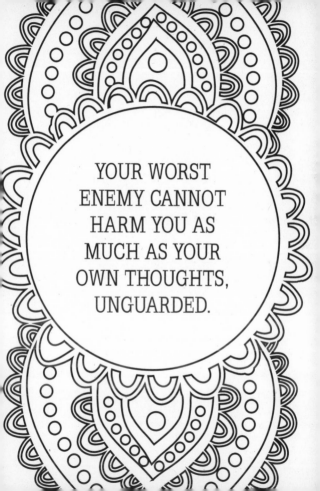

YOUR WORST
ENEMY CANNOT
HARM YOU AS
MUCH AS YOUR
OWN THOUGHTS,
UNGUARDED.

Long is the night to the sleepless;
long is the league to the weary.

Long is wordly existence to fools
who know not the Sublime Truth.

THERE IS NO FIRE
LIKE PASSION, NO
SEIZURE LIKE ANGER,
NO SNARE LIKE
DELUSION, NO RIVER
LIKE CRAVING.

Purity and impurity depend on oneself; no one can purify another.

To support mother and father, to cherish wife and children, and to be engaged in peaceful occupation – this is the greatest blessing.

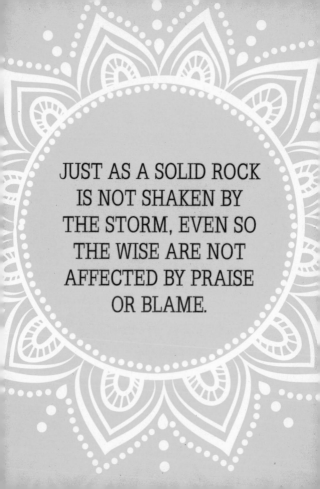

JUST AS A SOLID ROCK
IS NOT SHAKEN BY
THE STORM, EVEN SO
THE WISE ARE NOT
AFFECTED BY PRAISE
OR BLAME.

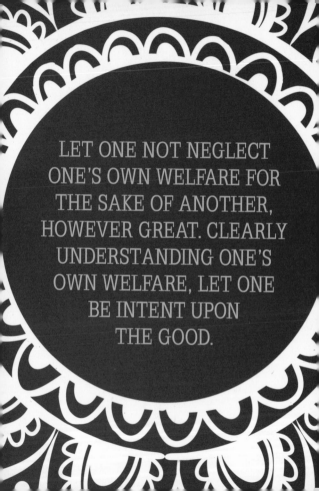

LET ONE NOT NEGLECT
ONE'S OWN WELFARE FOR
THE SAKE OF ANOTHER,
HOWEVER GREAT. CLEARLY
UNDERSTANDING ONE'S
OWN WELFARE, LET ONE
BE INTENT UPON
THE GOOD.

Searching all directions
with your awareness,
you find no one dearer
than yourself.
In the same way, others
are dear to themselves.
So you shouldn't hurt others
if you love yourself.

It is like a lighted torch whose flame can be distributed to ever so many other torches which people may bring along; and therewith they will cook food and dispel darkness, while the original torch itself remains burning ever the same. It is even so with the bliss of the Way.

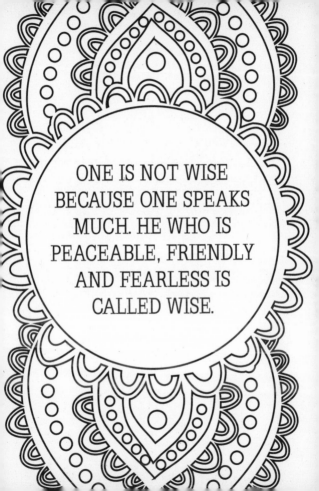

ONE IS NOT WISE
BECAUSE ONE SPEAKS
MUCH. HE WHO IS
PEACEABLE, FRIENDLY
AND FEARLESS IS
CALLED WISE.

All tremble at violence;
all fear death.

Putting oneself in the place of
another, one should not kill
nor cause another to kill.

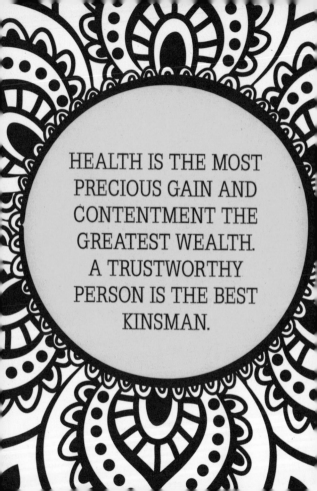

HEALTH IS THE MOST
PRECIOUS GAIN AND
CONTENTMENT THE
GREATEST WEALTH.
A TRUSTWORTHY
PERSON IS THE BEST
KINSMAN.

Whatever a monk keeps
pursuing with his thinking and
pondering, that becomes the
inclination of his awareness.

An act to make another happy,
inspires the other to make still
another happy, and so happiness
is aroused and abounds.

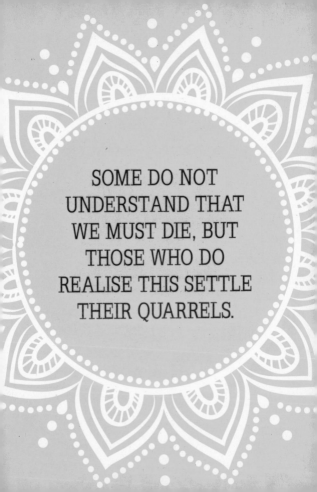

SOME DO NOT
UNDERSTAND THAT
WE MUST DIE, BUT
THOSE WHO DO
REALISE THIS SETTLE
THEIR QUARRELS.

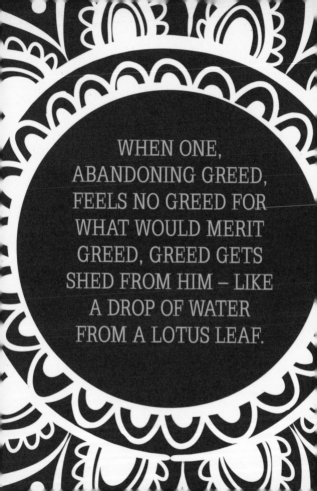

WHEN ONE, ABANDONING GREED, FEELS NO GREED FOR WHAT WOULD MERIT GREED, GREED GETS SHED FROM HIM – LIKE A DROP OF WATER FROM A LOTUS LEAF.

The mentor can be identified by four things: by restraining you from wrongdoing, guiding you towards good actions, telling you what you ought to know, and showing you the path to heaven.

In four ways… should one who flatters be understood as a foe in the guise of a friend: He approves of his friend's evil deeds, he disapproves his friend's good deeds, he praises him in his presence, he speaks ill of him in his absence.

ADMIRABLE
FRIENDSHIP, ADMIRABLE
COMPANIONSHIP,
ADMIRABLE CAMARADERIE
IS ACTUALLY THE WHOLE
OF THE HOLY LIFE.

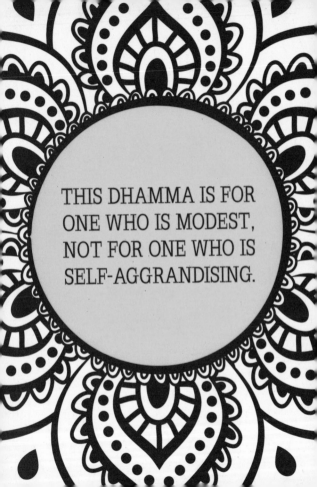

THIS DHAMMA IS FOR
ONE WHO IS MODEST,
NOT FOR ONE WHO IS
SELF-AGGRANDISING.

Those who don't discern stress,
what brings stress into play, and
where it totally stops, without
trace; who don't know the path,
the way to the stilling of stress…
they're headed to birth and aging.

Generosity, kind words, beneficial help, and consistency in the face of events, in line with what's appropriate in each case, each case. These bonds of fellowship [function] in the world like the linchpin in a moving cart.

WHEN YOU DWELL
WITH THE DOORS TO YOUR
SENSES WELL-GUARDED,
MARA, NOT GETTING ANY
OPPORTUNITY, WILL LOSE
INTEREST AND LEAVE,
JUST AS THE JACKAL DID
WITH THE TORTOISE.

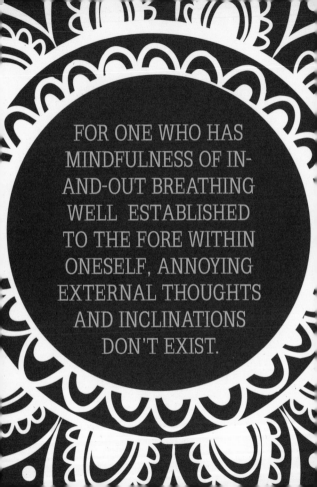

FOR ONE WHO HAS
MINDFULNESS OF IN-
AND-OUT BREATHING
WELL ESTABLISHED
TO THE FORE WITHIN
ONESELF, ANNOYING
EXTERNAL THOUGHTS
AND INCLINATIONS
DON'T EXIST.

At any time when a disciple of the noble ones is recollecting virtue, his mind is not overcome with passion, not overcome with aversion, not overcome with delusion. His mind heads straight, based on virtue.

If by renouncing a lesser
happiness one may realise
a greater happiness,

let the wise man renounce
the lesser, having regard
for the greater.

If you're interested in finding
out more about our books, find us on
Facebook at **Summersdale Publishers**
and follow us on Twitter at
@Summersdale.

www.summersdale.com